The Excellent Spirit

The Importance of Excellence in your Life

Jamal E. Quinn

ML Excellence Publishing

Table of Contents

DEDICATION

I dedicate this book first and foremost to Jesus Christ, my Lord and Savior. I also dedicate this to my mother, the late Mary L. Quinn who passed away at an early age. She was an amazing woman and had an excellent spirit. She had a love for music, and taught me the importance of excellence, education, music, honor, respect and to always do my best!

To all of my friends in my hometown, Louisville, Ky., the military, ministry and all over the world, and last but not least, to the young men and women who would read this book. I encourage you to do all things in a spirit of excellence and greatness will overtake you! May God bless you abundantly in Jesus' name!

INTRODUCTION

The scripture says in Proverbs 22:1, "A good name is rather to be chosen than great riches, and loving favor rather than silver and gold." As I thought about this scripture, I thought to myself, what truly makes a person's name great? We could say many things, such as education, because they have achieved great honors in academics. Because they are famous or well-known, because of who are they are, or what they have accomplished, or maybe they a good heart and wonderful personality that distinguishes them from others.

All of these things are good and could be correct, but understand that excellence sets you apart and your name represents who you are. When people say your name or talk about you, what do they say and what do they see? Understand that what you do, and how you do it, sets you apart from the crowd.

This is why you should do all things in a spirit of excellence. Because what you do, and how you do it, has your name attached to it. If whatever you do is done in a spirit of mediocrity, this is what people see and remember about you. Let's be real, nobody remembers failures, but they do remember winners! If you desire to set yourself apart from the crowd, do all things in a spirit of excellence, and people will remember your work and who you are! This book is written to anyone who desires to excel or be excellent in whatever they set their hands to do in life!

Why? Because what you do represents who you are and sets you apart from the crowd! Never allow mediocrity to be your portion. Remember to do all things in a spirit of excellence, having the right attitude and people will remember your work and who you are!

CHAPTER 1

What is Excellence?

If you asked someone the definition of excellence, you would probably get a variety of responses. My personal definition would be that it is the state of something that is outstanding and set apart from good, better or best. The dictionary defines it as; the quality of being outstanding or extremely good. Other words or synonyms that describe excellence are; distinction, quality, high quality, superiority, brilliance, greatness, merit, caliber, eminence, preeminence, value, worth, skill, talent, genius, accomplishment, mastery and ability.

All of these definitions definitely describe what excellence is or should consist of. Excellence is something that stands out. The opposite of excellence is mediocre, lack of quality, inferior, imperfection, failure, flawed, shortcoming, average, insignificant, pettiness, cheap, lack of, shoddy, trivial, or insufficient.

Now think with me for a moment. Which one of these definitions describe your life and everything that you do? You see, excellence is something that we should desire in everything that we do. Excellence is not education, but can be achieved through education, excellence is not intelligence, but involves intelligence. Excellence is not experience, but experience can produce excellence. Excellence is something that every person should attain to achieve. There is nothing more dissatisfying than a person who does not do their best. I mean, when people see the work you do, what is the response? Do you do your best, or just do what you can? I was told many years ago in the military that, "First impressions are a lasting impression."

In the times that we live, we have access to information 24 hours a day. There is so much information out there where we can research a thing, and put our best foot forward to do our very best. There are so many examples of people who started at the bottom and made their way to the top, and they understood that cutting corners was not an option.

Why? Because excellence means you go the extra mile to ensure what you represent is the best, because mediocrity is not the standard. Anyone can do something and say, "Ok, I did it." The question is, "Did you do your best, and did you go the extra mile to accomplish and achieve it?" Excellence says, I put extra effort into it, because I want it to stand out above and beyond what is average!

Excellence says this is my best. Excellence says, this is top notch. Excellence says, "I do my best because my name is attached to it." When people see the excellent work you have done, they will marvel because it was done above and beyond the standard.

As you read this book, be mindful that each and every one of us has the ability to do our very best. Keep in mind that we all have different levels of ability, and if your very best is what you have, or can give, it is acceptable if it is your best effort!

To everyone who reads this book, I want to encourage you to go above and beyond the standard and the norm. I want to encourage you to be the best you can be in all you do. Excellence is important because what we do has our name attached to it, and we want to do our very best, setting a standard for all to follow!

CHAPTER 2

Excellence, Attitude and Discipline

Someone may be asking the question, "Why is excellence important in my life? Excellence is important because it sets a standard for all to follow. Let's take athletics for example. When you look at all the great athletes in the world today, or in the past, they have set a standard for all to follow in discipline.

I have found in my life that excellence and discipline go hand in hand. When you look at those who have achieved high degrees in education, and those that have set themselves apart in college, military, ministry and other careers achieving great things. It was because they had an excellence spirit, the right attitude and they were disciplined!

Excellence is important because people will remember what you did and what you accomplished for many years. No one follows anyone who is mediocre, lazy, or complacent. People tend to follow those that make a difference, or have accomplished great exploits, setting the standard for excellence.

Someone may be asking, "What do you know about excellence?" Well, allow me to share a quick testimony. When I think about my mother who passed away at the early age of 28. I remember her teaching me so many things.

I spend a lot of time with her because I had a medical condition as a child, and experienced firsthand a woman who was truly excellent. I remember when she went to the hospital when she was pregnant with my baby sister, she gave me some household instructions.

She told me to make sure I kept the house in order while she was away. So, from a young man at the age of eight years old, I began to do things at an early age that most young people don't do. I began to help clean the house, vacuum, and wash dishes as best as I could. I learned how to sew. I ironed my brothers' clothes before school and made sure they were pressed very good. I cleaned the kitchen and bathrooms until they were spotless, and even looked after my young brother and sister!

While in the hospital, my mother passed away from some medical complications. Although, my mother never came home and my heart was broken. It was my heart's desire to fulfill my mother's request that prompted me to do everything in excellence according to her wishes, following her example!

This attitude of doing things in excellence carried over into high school in academics and athletics. Although I graduated a year later, and didn't go to college right away, I performed very well with my grades! The attitude of excellence carried over into the military where I served for 21 years, and enabled me to get good evaluations, 20 years good conduct of service, the best duty stations, promotions, and many awards and medals throughout my career, because I wanted to do all things in excellence!

When I served in the U.S. Navy, I had the mindset to do things the right way. The military taught me discipline, how to be sharp and squared away in appearance, uniform and attitude.

One of the first things I learned quickly in the military is that first impressions are lasting impressions! The first impression that people get of you is a lasting impression. This is why you should carry yourself in an excellent way at all times. Never forget this! First impressions are lasting impressions. It doesn't matter whether you are interviewing for a job, trying out for a sport, going for a promotion, going on a date, starting a business, meeting someone for the first time, or starting a ministry.

Whatever you do, do it in the spirit of excellence! Never, ever do anything with a lackadaisical attitude. If you do, you will not succeed! Unfortunately, I can tell you many people I knew in the military found it hard to understand the importance of attitude and discipline, and did not succeed in the military. You see, excellence is about discipline. It is about consistency, and it is about setting a high standard to follow which is not the norm!

Excellence is also about attitude! There is no way you can be excellent with a negative, disobedient, rebellious, selfish, undisciplined, angry attitude. When I served in the military, I met people from all over the United States and around the world. Shout out to all my friends, brothers and sisters I met in the military around the world!

Excellence can come from ability as well. There are some people who were born with certain skillsets to accomplish great things, but the attitude to succeed, can outweigh ability if the desire is there!

I have also met people in the military and ministry with ability, but their attitude was not good. Therefore, they did not succeed. I have also met people who did not have ability, but they had an excellent attitude that was above and beyond their ability! Guess what? They succeeded!

Excellence is important because whatever you do has your name attached to it. Yes, we all make mistakes in life, but we should learn from those mistakes and turn our mistakes into excellence!

The attitude of excellence carried over into ministry when I volunteered and assisted Chaplains in the Navy. Because of my desire to do things in excellence with the right attitude, I was allowed to lead Sunday Gospel services on the ship. When I retired from the Navy, I started a group Bible study by faith, and later an independent non-denominational church that has blessed and changed many lives.

One of the things we must remember is that people will remember your achievements, but they will also remember the attitude you had as well! Attitude and discipline go hand in hand and will always result in a spirit of excellence.

When we talk about excellence, attitude, and discipline. We cannot leave out the most important virtue which is faithfulness. Listen to the testimony of a man named Daniel in scripture. Let's read!

Daniel 6:3-4
3 Then this Daniel distinguished himself above the presidents and princes, **because an excellent spirit was in him;** and the king gave thought to setting him over the whole realm.
4 So the presidents and princes sought to find some charge against Daniel concerning the kingdom; **but they could find no charge or fault, because he was faithful;** nor was there any error or fault found in him.

As we can see, excellence and faithfulness go together. If you are going to be excellent, you must be faithful in all that you do! Listen to what the Paul the Apostle tells a young man named Timothy in the scriptures! Let's read 2 Timothy chapter 2, verse 2-7!

2Tim 2:2 And the things that you have heard from me among many witnesses, **commit these to faithful men who will be able to teach others also.**
2Tim 2:3 You therefore must endure hardship as a good soldier of Jesus Christ.
2Tim 2:4 No one engaged in warfare entangles himself with the affairs of this life, that he may please him who enlisted him as a soldier.
2Tim 2:5 And also if anyone competes in athletics, he is not crowned unless he competes according to the rules.
2Tim 2:6 The hardworking farmer must be first to partake of the crops.
2Tim 2:7 Consider what I say, and may the Lord give you understanding in all things.

Notice that Paul tells Timothy, to commit these things to faithful men, who will teach others also! Consider these statements!

1. Faithfulness is something that many people lack today. If you are not faithful in what has been committed to you, you lack excellence. Always, remember to be faithful in whatever you have been assigned or committed to do. When you are faithful, people will favor you and commit more responsibility to you.

2. Paul also said to endure hardship.
Sometimes when you are doing things in excellence it calls for hard work in which you have to endure

16

hardship. Remember everything nice in life, has a price and a sacrifice! One of the things I tell young people is that when you work hard, you will reap the benefits of it. Don't expect to be great, and be mediocre in how you work towards your goals! **Remember, the only place success comes before work is in the dictionary!**

The wise man Solomon said in Proverbs 22:1, "A good name is to be chosen rather than great riches, loving favor rather than silver and gold."

Whatever you do, has your name assigned to it. It is your work. It is your accomplishment. The question is, "Do you want to be remembered for the excellence that you do, or the lack of excellence thereof?"

3. **Paul then talks about a soldier, an athlete and a farmer.** What do they all have in common? I'm glad you asked!

Well, they all work hard and have discipline. They get up early, and they are faithful in what they do. They have a goal in mind, and they understand that in order to succeed, they must do everything in excellence! Consider this:

A soldier cannot be slack. Their uniforms must be ironed, creased and sharp. They must have the right attitude, they must be on time, and disciplined!

An athlete cannot be slack as well. They must work hard to accomplish their goals, which involves training discipline and the right attitude. You cannot win the gold or the trophy if you do not work hard, have the right attitude, and go the extra mile with discipline!

A farmer cannot be slack as well. In order to reap a harvest from his labor, he must be disciplined and consistent day in and day out. He must have the right attitude to get up early consistently, work hard, and ensure his crops are the best on the market to sell!

You must have the right attitude and discipline as well! You will not do great things in the times we live today without the right attitude and discipline!

Excellence in character is also important. I heard someone once say, reputation is what people think of you. Character is who you really are! Excellence is embodied in character. Your attitude, mindset and personality are important as it relates to excellence!

Being honest, treating people right, and having genuine love in your heart embodies the spirit of excellence. Remember that your attitude and discipline are important as it relates to excellence!

CHAPTER 3

The LORD is Excellent!

To the Chief musician upon Gittith, a Psalm of David.
O LORD, our Lord, How excellent is Your name in all
the earth, who have set Your glory above the
heavens!
(Psalm 8:1 NKJV)

Did you know that God is excellent in all his ways?
There is no way we can talk about excellence without
mentioning the excellence of God (Elohim).
Everything the LORD has created is excellent,
because his standard is excellence! There is nothing
that God has created that is not good! That's why in
Genesis after he created the heavens and the earth,
the creatures of the air, earth and sea, the scriptures
record, "And God saw that it was good." (Gen 1:12,
18, 21, 25 and 31)

God is so excellent when we gave Moses the
instructions to build the Tabernacle, a place he would
dwell among his people, he told Moses in Exodus
25:9, " According to all that I show you, after the
pattern of the tabernacle, and the pattern of all the
instruments thereof, even so shall you make it."

In other words, Moses, "I want you to make it just as
I showed you. Do not deviate from the pattern. Why?

Because I am excellent in all my ways, and what I am showing you is perfect. The Bible records that God reminded Moses to make it according to the pattern.

One of the things we must understand about the Most High God is that his character and attributes are excellent. King David the man, who the Bible says was after God's heart, said the following about him:

"O LORD, our Lord, How excellent is your name in all the earth, who have set Your glory above the heavens!" (Psalm 8:1)

He goes on to say in Psalm 8:3, "When I consider Your heavens, the work of Your fingers, the moon and the stars, which You have ordained."

David thought about the goodness and greatness of God, and considered all the wonderful things that he created, and wrote a Psalm about the excellence of God!

There is no other name in all the earth as excellent as the LORD, who created the heavens and the earth! If God himself is excellent and we were created in his image, then we should follow his example in excellence as well!

Someone once said, "I am careful not to confuse excellence with perfection. Excellence I can reach for; perfection is God's business."

That really sums it up! Excellence is not perfection, but excellence is something we can all obtain, even if we never reach perfection! God in his great grace allows us to strive for excellence, but because of sin, and the flesh, sometimes it is hard to achieve. Excellence is within our grasp, because we all have the ability to strive for excellence, and to raise the standard in all that we do.

When we think about the character of God and the standards that he sets for his people, it is all about doing things in excellence and order. God does not lower his standards for us, but he does give us grace! Nevertheless, we must come up to that standard. Consider the following statements:

1. Gods' standard is excellence, because he is excellent.
2. Gods' standard is righteousness, and we must be righteous.
3. Gods' standard is holiness, and we must be holy.
4. Gods' standard is truth, and we must abide by truth.
5. Gods' standard is servitude, and we must serve in order to be great.
6. Gods' standard is faithfulness, and we must be faithful.
7. God's standard is love, and we must walk in love!

God sets a standard in character and excellence, and we are called to live by that standard!

There are many quotes on excellence, but my favorite is:

"When you have had a taste of excellence, you cannot go back to mediocrity." Maximillian Degenerez

When we desire the standard of excellence we do our very best. We go the extra mile, and we work hard to achieve the goal of excellence!

Yes, God understands who you are, and where you are, but never underestimate your ability to go higher, to go deeper, and to do your very best to set a standard for all to follow.

Earlier in the chapter we mentioned when God gave Moses the blueprint of the Tabernacle. He told him several times, "Make sure you build it according to the pattern I showed you." Why? Because when God gives us a perfect example or standard, we must follow it. Because we know that God has the pattern of excellence for us to follow.

When we follow his example according to the Word, we will have good success in all of our endeavors. Look at the number of times the scripture mentions what the LORD told Moses about following his example!

Exo 25:9 According to all that I show you, that is, the pattern of the tabernacle and the pattern of all its furnishings, just so you shall make it.

Exo 25:40 And see to it that you make them according to the pattern which was shown you on the mountain.

Exo 26:30 And you shall raise up the tabernacle according to its pattern which you were shown on the mountain.

Num 8:4 Now this workmanship of the lampstand was hammered gold; from its shaft to its flowers, it was hammered work. According to the pattern which the LORD had shown Moses, so he made the lampstand.

Act 7:44 "Our fathers had the tabernacle of witness in the wilderness, as He appointed, instructing Moses to make it according to the pattern that he had seen."

Heb 8:5 who serve the copy and shadow of the heavenly things, as Moses was divinely instructed when he was about to make the tabernacle. For He said, "See that you make all things according to the pattern shown you on the mountain."

Isn't it interesting that the scripture mentions this multiple times? The reason being is that it shows us that God has a standard and a pattern of excellence that we should not deviate from. What he has given us and shows us cannot be duplicated by any human being, but we can follow his word and his pattern to be excellent in all that we do!

Young people today follow examples that may be a trend, or a fad, or something that is temporary. The excellence of God in your life sets you apart from anything that man could ever create or come up with.

God is set apart in all his ways and everything he has ordained and created is good and excellent. So, when we seek after God and follow the pattern in scripture that he has set for us, we too will become an example and a pattern for all to follow!

The Word of God says in James 1:17, "Every good gift and every perfect gift is from above, and comes down from the Father of lights, with whom there is no variation or shadow of turning."

God is good and everything he does is good and excellent. James said that every good and perfect gift comes from God. King David understood this and gave glory and praise to God in Psalm 150, because of his excellent greatness!

"Praise him for his mighty acts: praise him according to his excellent greatness." (Psalms 150:2 KJV)

In the book of Job, listen to what the oldest book in the Bible says about the excellence of God.

Touching the Almighty, we cannot find him out: he is excellent in power, and in judgment, and in plenty of justice: he will not afflict.
(Job 37:23 KJV)

Job says that even though we know God, we cannot truly comprehend his excellence. Why? Because he is truly excellent in power, judgment and justice.

In other words, there is an excellence about the LORD that we cannot truly understand. There is absolutely nothing in God that is lacking. This is why he is God Almighty which is translated as "El Shaddai" in the Hebrew.

There are other scriptures that speak of the LORD's excellence as well!

How excellent is thy lovingkindness, O God! therefore the children of men put their trust under the shadow of thy wings.
(Psalms 36:7 KJV)

You are more glorious and excellent than the mountains of prey.
(Psalms 76:4 NKJV)

Let them praise the name of the LORD: for his name alone is excellent; his glory is above the earth and heaven.
(Psalms 148:13 KJV)

Sing to the LORD, For He has done excellent things; This is known in all the earth.
(Isaiah 12:5 NKJV)

As we see in scripture, the LORD is excellent in all his ways, and since we are made in his image. We should desire to know him for who he is, and follow his example of excellence, in all that he has done in the earth.

CHAPTER 4

Daniel: An Example of Excellence

Forasmuch as an excellent spirit, and knowledge, and understanding, interpreting of dreams, and showing of hard sentences, and dissolving of doubts, were found in the same Daniel, whom the king named Belteshazzar: now let Daniel be called, and he will shew the interpretation.
(Daniel 5:12 KJV)

When I think about examples of excellence in the bible, there is one specific person that comes to mind besides the LORD Jesus Christ, and that is the Prophet Daniel. Before we talk about his life and the excellent spirit that he had. Let's look at his life and the testimony of the excellent spirit he had!

Daniel was of the tribe of Judah and lived in Jerusalem. Biblical history states that in the 6th century BC, Nebuchadnezzar of Babylon invaded Jerusalem as God prophesied in Jeremiah chapter 25.

The scripture says that he took many of the Hebrews captive according to Biblical history. When we read the story, we find there are some important life lessons in excellence that we can learn from! Listen to the scriptures in the book of Daniel. Let's read!

Dan 1:1 In the third year of the reign of Jehoiakim king of Judah, Nebuchadnezzar king of Babylon came to Jerusalem and besieged it.

Dan 1:2 And the Lord gave Jehoiakim king of Judah into his hand, with some of the articles of the house of God, which he carried into the land of Shinar to the house of his god; and he brought the articles into the treasure house of his god.

Dan 1:3 Then the king instructed Ashpenaz, the master of his eunuchs, to bring some of the children of Israel and some of the king's descendants and some of the nobles,

Dan 1:4 young men in whom there was no blemish, but good-looking, gifted in all wisdom, possessing knowledge and quick to understand, who had ability to serve in the king's palace, and whom they might teach the language and literature of the Chaldeans.

So, after Jerusalem was invaded and Judah taken captive. There were many Hebrews that went into captivity. Daniel was a young man probably between the ages fifteen and twenty years old, and although he was a young man, Daniel had an excellent spirit.

So, you may ask, what was it about him that was excellent? Well, let's take a look! After Judah was taken captive as slaves. Many of the young men were forced into an indoctrination program in the Babylonian society.

The King's plan was to feed them their food, their wine, and give them a worldly secular Babylonian education.

What is interesting is that Daniel rejected this. The Bible says that Daniel purposed in his heart that he would not defile himself in Daniel 1:8.

"But Daniel purposed in his heart that he would not defile himself with the portion of the king's delicacies, nor with the wine which he drank; therefore, he requested of the chief of the eunuchs that he might not defile himself."
(Daniel 1:8 NKJV)

There are some things we can learn from the Daniels' excellent attitude and spirit!

Key number 1 to having an excellent spirit.
The very first thing in achieving excellence in your life is that you must purpose some things in your heart?

When you understand that you have purpose, you will purpose in your heart certain things about your life. Such as, where you will go, what you will watch, who you will hang out with, what you will say, and above all that you are not going to follow the crowd.

Do you know why some people can't achieve excellence in your lives? They haven't purposed some things in their heart.

They are still undecided in purpose, and haven't made the decision to stand on the promises of God, no matter what comes their way.

You see, it takes heart to reject certain things that don't line up with your purpose and vision. But you have got to purpose in your heart no matter what everybody else is doing, you will not become a part of it.

In other words, Daniel didn't compromise who he was in the LORD. Daniel said, I might be a slave physically, but I'm a child of God spiritually and mentally! Daniel was a Hebrew and there were certain things that he would not eat or do. In other words, he was steadfast and disciplined!

Key number 2 to having an excellent spirit. You must have discipline. Some people are just so undisciplined. You must discipline yourself spiritually, physically, mentally, financially and personally. You must be disciplined in prayer, disciplined in the study of the word, disciplined in your work, and above all, you must discipline your mouth. Every area in your life must be disciplined if you are going to have an excellent spirit. If we do not discipline ourselves, it will be hard to maintain an excellent spirit.

Key number 3 to having an excellent spirit. You must represent yourself well. You can tell people that have an excellent spirit, because of the way they carry themselves. Not prideful, but humble and kind. Also, excellent individuals have a good testimony among many. Everyone may not like you, but they will respect you! Not only that, you must represent the LORD well. Not only in church, but on your job, in your school and wherever you go.

Proverbs 22:1 says, "A good name is rather to be chosen than great riches, and loving favor rather than silver and gold."

What is amazing about Daniel is that although he was a slave, the people in Babylon knew who he was!

In Daniel chapter 5, the story is recorded of King Belshazzar, the son of King Nebuchadnezzar of Babylon who had a party and a great feast. During this party he received a prophecy of death from the LORD because of his pride. Let's read!

Dan 5:3 Then they brought the gold vessels that had been taken from the temple of the house of God which had been in Jerusalem; and the king and his lords, his wives, and his concubines drank from them.

Dan 5:4 They drank wine, and praised the gods of gold and silver, bronze and iron, wood and stone.

Dan 5:5 In the same hour the fingers of a man's hand appeared and wrote opposite the lampstand on the plaster of the wall of the king's palace; and the king saw the part of the hand that wrote.

In other words, God himself told him that his time was up because of his pride and disrespect for the things of the temple that belonged to God!

The King was terrified of what he saw. So, he called all of his astrologers and soothsayers in to read it, but none could give the interpretation.

The scripture says that all the king's wise men came, but they could not read the writing, or make known to the king its interpretation.
(Daniel 5:8 NKJV)

But then someone remembered a young man named Daniel, who was excellent in thought, words and deeds. Listen to what they said about him. This is powerful!

Dan 5:11 There is a man in your kingdom in whom is the Spirit of the Holy God. And in the days of your father, light and understanding and wisdom, like the wisdom of the gods, were found in him; and King Nebuchadnezzar your father—your father the king— made him chief of the magicians, astrologers, Chaldeans, and soothsayers.

Dan 5:12 Inasmuch as an excellent spirit, knowledge, understanding, interpreting dreams, solving riddles, and explaining

enigmas were found in this Daniel, whom the king named Belteshazzar, now let Daniel be called, and he will give the interpretation."

So, they brought in the Prophet Daniel to interpret the prophetic word because someone remembered that this was an excellent young man. Listen to what they said about Daniel!

Dan 5:13 Then Daniel was brought in before the king. The king spoke, and said to Daniel, "Are you that Daniel who is one of the captives from Judah, whom my father the king brought from Judah?

Dan 5:14 I have heard of you, that the Spirit of God is in you, and **that light and understanding and excellent wisdom are found in you.**

Did you hear what the people (outsiders) said about him? Listen, there are people who know you and don't know you, but the question is do you have an excellent spirit?

To make a long story short. Daniel was able to read the interpretation because he served the LORD, and God gifted him with prophetic ability to interpret the prophecy. After he interpreted the prophecy, look how they rewarded him.

Dan 5:29 Then Belshazzar gave the command, and they clothed Daniel with purple, and put a chain of gold around his neck, and made a proclamation concerning him that he should be the third ruler in the kingdom.

Did you hear that? Because he had an excellent spirit, they gave him a purple robe which is a symbol and garment of royalty, and they put a gold chain on his neck. Not only that, but they promoted him! This is a powerful testimony of excellence!

Key number 4. When you have an excellent spirit you set yourself up for promotion. People that have an excellent spirit are the ones that get promoted because of their reputation of doing things in excellence.

Key number 5. You will never have good success and promotion without having an excellent spirit!

When you continue to read the book of Daniel the Prophet, you will find that he continued to have a good testimony, they promoted him again, and he was recognized for his excellence in the Babylonian kingdom as a Hebrew. Let's read!

Dan 6:1 It pleased Darius to set over the kingdom one hundred and twenty princes, to be over the whole kingdom;
Dan 6:2 and over these, three governors, of whom Daniel was one, that the princes might give account to them, so that the king would suffer no loss.

Dan 6:3 **Then this Daniel distinguished himself above the governors and princes, because an excellent spirit was in him; and the king gave thought to setting him over the whole realm.**

Dan 6:4 So the governors and princes sought to find some charge against Daniel concerning the kingdom; but they could find no charge or fault, because he was faithful; nor was there any error or fault found in him.

Isn't that amazing? Daniel was promoted in the Kingdom because he had an **excellent spirit**. The scripture says that he distinguished himself above the governors and princes, because an excellent spirit was in him, and the king gave thought to setting him over the whole realm!

When you have an excellent spirit, sometimes it will bring the haters out of the woodwork. But don't worry, God has your back! They tried to find fault against Daniel but could not find a charge or fault, Why? Because he was faithful.

Key number 6. People with an excellent spirit are faithful and have a good testimony.

What we read from the scriptures is a young man that would not compromise who he was. He was excellent, he was faithful, and because of his testimony he was promoted!

I want to say to someone reading this story. God is not a respecter of persons. Excellence in your life will open doors on your behalf. It will cause you to be noticed. It will also promote you. Someone once said, "Great people do little things with excellence."

No matter what task you are assigned. Do it with excellence. Do it to the best of your ability and you will shine. Daniels's testimony is truly an example for all to follow. Never forget who you are and who you represent!

When you do all things in excellence you set yourself apart from the crowd and great opportunities will be yours!

CHAPTER 5

Excellence in Scripture

Someone may be asking, is excellence really that important? In this chapter we are going to look at scriptures on excellence to see what the Bible has to say about it.

Whether you read the Bible or not doesn't matter. Excellence is for anyone that desires to be at the top of their game, and it will set you apart from everyone else.

So, let's take a look at what the scripture says about excellence in your life, and those that have an excellent spirit. Let's read!

"As for the saints who are in the earth, "They are the excellent ones, in whom is all my delight."
(Psalms 16:3 NKJV)

Again, David shows us that he is of an excellent spirit and uses the word quite often in the Psalms. In Psalm 16, he speaks a word about the saints who are in the earth. He refers to them as the excellent ones in whom is all the LORD's delight.

We see that excellence will always set you apart. It will identify you as unique, and put you in a different category than everyone else.

One thing I have found about excellent people is that they have an excellent spirit, an excellent attitude, and an excellent work ethic. When you find someone who is truly of an excellent spirit, you will find that there is something about them that sets them apart from others. Listen to the scriptures!

He that has knowledge spares his words: and a man of understanding is of an excellent spirit.
(Proverbs 17:27 KJV)

In the times that we live with social media people are not very quiet. Why? Because everyone has something to say whether foolish or wise! There is nothing wrong with self-expression, but the Bible says that an individual that spares his words has knowledge! It is a true saying that when you don't have much to say, people wonder about you. I have personally learned that silent can be golden!

Wisdom tells us to be slow to speak and quick to listen. So, we must use wisdom to observe, watch and pray. The Word of God also says that wisdom is the principal thing, and in all your getting, get understanding.

Wisdom is the principal thing; Therefore, get wisdom, and in all your getting, get understanding.
(Proverbs 4:7 NKJV)

A person who has understanding is one who has an excellent spirit according to Proverbs 17:27.

The word understanding in the Hebrew is "tebuna" or "towbunah" and is translated as intelligence, discretion, reason, skillfulness, or wisdom in the *Strong's Talking Greek & Hebrew Dictionary.*

So, a man or woman who has understanding is one who has discretion, reason, skillful, has wisdom and intelligence.

David said in Psalms 8:1, "O LORD, our Lord, How excellent is Your name in all the earth, Who have set Your glory above the heavens!"

The word excellent in Psalms 8:1 is "adder" which is translated as glorious, goodly, lordly, mighty, noble, principal, and worthy. *Strong's Talking Greek & Hebrew Dictionary.*

Isn't the Most High God noble, mighty, glorious and worthy? He also possesses absolute intelligence, reason and supreme wisdom!

So, when we follow the example of excellence, we are identifying with our creator who is the possessor of all things that pertain to wisdom, knowledge, and understanding!

Another attribute of God is love. David tells us in Psalm 36 that God's lovingkindness is excellent! He uses two words to express this; loving and kindness. These two words express the character of God and how he deals with his people.

Let's take a look at the scripture!

How excellent is your lovingkindness, O God!
therefore the children of men put their trust under
the shadow of thy wings.
(Psalms 36:7 KJV)

God is indeed love and shows us kindness, and he is
excellent indeed! This is an example that we can all
follow! Because love is the greatest commandment,
and when we walk in excellent love, we exemplify the
character of Christ.

Paul the Apostle wrote about the excellence of love as
well in 1 Corinthians chapter 12.

But earnestly desire the best gifts. And yet I show you
a more excellent way.
(1 Corinthians 12:31 NKJV)

What was the excellent way that he was referring to?
It was the way of love. If you read in 1 Corinthians 13,
you will find that he expounds on the importance of
love in great detail. The excellent way of love and
kindness is something that many people have not
ascribed too, even in the church!

This is why we have division, racism, discord and so
many other things that plaque our churches,
communities, cities and country. It is amazing that
we talk about love, and say we know the one who has

excellent love. Yet, we find it hard to express excellent love to one another. (Selah)

Remember the words of Christ in John chapter 13.

A new commandment I give to you, that you love one another; as I have loved you, that you also love one another.
(John 13:34 NKJV)

There is another scripture in 2 Peter in which he refers to love and kindness as well. He mentions them because we all need certain virtues that will enable us to represent God in excellence.

2 Peter 1:5-8 NKJV
(5) But also, for this very reason, giving all diligence, add to your faith virtue, to virtue knowledge,
(6) to knowledge self-control, to self-control perseverance, to perseverance godliness,
(7) to godliness brotherly kindness, and to brotherly kindness love.
(8) For if these things are yours and abound, you will be neither barren nor unfruitful in the knowledge of our Lord Jesus Christ.

Notice that verse 7 mentions brotherly kindness and brotherly love. Remember David in referring to the LORD said:

How excellent is your lovingkindness, O God!
therefore the children of men put their trust under
the shadow of thy wings.
(Psalms 36:7 KJV)

Love and kindness are excellent virtues that everyone
needs. These two virtues exemplify the character of
Christ. There is no way one can say they have the
spirit of God, and not reflect the loving-kindness of
God that David refers to in Psalm 36.

Last, but not least, we put our trust in God because of
his loving kindness which is truly excellent. Let us
reflect on these two virtues and never let them cease
or depart from our life!

CHAPTER 6

The Importance of Excellence in your Life

We have shared on many things as it relates to excellence. Now the most important question we ask is, "Why is excellence important in my life?"

Well, from a biblical perspective it is important because first and foremost, we serve the LORD who is excellent in all his ways, and when we do things in a spirit of excellence, we represent not only ourselves, but the LORD.

The Word of God tells us to let our light shine that others may see our good works and glorify God in heaven.

"Let your light so shine before men, that they may see your good works and glorify your Father in heaven." Matthew 5:16

Living an excellent life in Christ is important for us because as Kingdom citizens in Christ, we represent the King of Kings and Lord of Lords in the earth. As representatives in the earth, we are ambassadors for Christ! We live in a time today where people follow trends, fads, and what is popular in culture, but we should always set the example for others to follow as the light of the world!

Why? Because we serve an excellent God, and since we have his spirit, we should be excellent in all of our ways!

If you aren't doing all things in a spirit of excellence, you may be slacking in your excellence for the LORD! Why? Because the scripture tells us that whatever we do, do it as unto the LORD!

Col 3:17 And whatever you do in word or deed, do all in the name of the Lord Jesus, giving thanks to God the Father through Him.
Col 3:23 And whatever you do, do it heartily, as to the Lord and not to men,
Col 3:24 knowing that from the Lord you will receive the reward of the inheritance; for you serve the Lord Christ.

Who did Paul say we serve? The Lord Christ!
You see, the LORD is not looking for the most anointed individual. He is looking for a willing vessel who will represent him and bring glory to his name!

When you think about the people God used in the Bible. They were not perfect. Moses was not the most anointed, and had a stuttering problem. But God still used him. Gideon was a hiding from the enemy, but God called him a mighty man of valor and used him!

As children of the Most High God, excellence should be a characteristic of the people of God.

It's amazing that people will give their employers more productivity and excellence on the job, than they give to God! But understand, God deserves our very best in all that we do!

Here are some questions to ponder considering excellence in your life!

1. Is excellence important to me?
2. Do I represent Jesus Christ in all that I do and wherever I go?
3. Am I excellent in my service to others?

All believers who serve and represent Christ should live a life of excellence. It doesn't matter how old or young you are, or how long you have been saved! We are all called to excellence!

In the book of Daniel, God was pleased with the Prophet Daniel, and we read something interesting about him. Listen to the angel of the LORD's testimony about Daniel in scripture!

Dan 9:23 At the beginning of thy supplications the commandment came forth, and I am come to shew thee; **for you are greatly beloved**: therefore, understand the matter, and consider the vision.

Dan 10:11 **And he said unto me, O Daniel, a man greatly beloved**, understand the words that I speak unto you, and stand upright: for unto you am I now sent. And when he had spoken this word unto me, I stood trembling.

Dan 10:19 **And said, O man greatly beloved, fear not: peace be unto thee, be strong, yea, be strong.** And when he had spoken unto me, I was strengthened, and said, Let my lord speak; for thou hast strengthened me.

Daniel was referred to as beloved in the sight of the LORD. I am sure that his excellent spirit and unwavering love for God was part of the reason!

Remember what David said again in Psalm 16:3, " As for the saints who are on the earth, "They are the excellent ones, in whom is all my delight."

Did you hear that? The LORD said that the excellent ones are his delight! If you are an excellent one, it means you have an awesome testimony before the LORD!

When we look at the excellent testimony of Jesus Christ, our Heavenly Father told him:

Luke 3:21-22
21 When all the people were baptized, it came to pass that Jesus also was baptized; and while He prayed, the heaven was opened.
22 And the Holy Spirit descended in bodily form like a dove upon Him, and a voice came from heaven

which said, **"You are My beloved Son; in You I am well pleased."**

Why was Jesus' beloved in the sight of the LORD? I believe because of his obedience, faithfulness, humility, servitude and above all. The excellence attitude that he had, in everything he did for Father God.

Understand as a believer in Christ, if you are not following the example of one of the greatest leaders that ever walked this earth, who is Jesus Christ, then you may not have the spirit of excellence.

So, if we are the excellent ones according to Psalm 16:3, who are God's delight, we should dress excellent, speak excellent, serve excellent, and do all things in excellence unto the LORD!

Above all, always be faithful and take care of anything that has been committed to your care with excellence! Anything else is unacceptable! If you are not sure what excellence looks like, look at the life of Jesus Christ. His character, his leadership, his prayer life, and his love for people was truly excellent!

We should always reflect the attributes of our Lord Jesus Christ in everything we say, wherever we work, wherever we live, and whatever we do. Remember to always do your best in a spirit of excellence!

CHAPTER 7

Living a Life of Excellence

"But we have this treasure in earthen vessels, that the excellence of the power may be of God and not of us." (2 Corinthians 4:7)

In the Old and New Testament there are about thirty-four verses of scripture in the Bible concerning the word excellent! Most of them speak of the excellent nature of God, and some of them speak of the excellent attitude that we should have.

I find this to be interesting because if we are to be excellent in all that we do, we must follow the example of Christ, and the example of excellence in scripture. Now understand, excellence for us doesn't mean perfection but it does mean we are striving for it!

The Word of God says in 1 Peter 2:9 that we are a royal priesthood, a holy nation, and a peculiar people. Peculiar means; strange, odd, unusual, out of the ordinary, exceptional, extraordinary, remarkable, puzzling, or mysterious.

Does that describe anybody reading this book? Well, it should, because we are to be excellent saints in Jesus' name!

Remember Psalm 16:3 says, "As for the saints who are on the earth, "They are the excellent ones, in whom is all my delight."

I want to remind you that are a Kingdom citizen in Christ, an ambassador for Christ, and that your citizenship is in heaven!

Remember Colossians 1:13 says you have been translated into the Kingdom of the LORD's dear Son!

So, if your citizenship is in heaven, and you are an ambassador for Christ, you have been called to live an excellent holy life in Jesus' name. When we live an excellent life in Christ, we bring glory to God in all that we do!

As a matter of fact, excellent saints who follow the example of Christ must have a humble spirit, be obedient to the Word, have an attitude of servitude and most importantly, love one another as God loves us.

Someone once said, "Excellence is not a skill, it is an attitude!" So, if this is true, excellence starts with the right attitude and having the right mindset. The Apostle Paul gives us wisdom in scripture which will enable us to have the right attitude and mindset as it relates to excellence!

"Finally, brethren, whatever things are true, whatever things are noble, whatever things are just, whatever things are pure, whatever things are lovely, whatever things are of good report, if there is any virtue and if there is anything praiseworthy—meditate on these things." (Philippians 4:8)

So, the question is what are you meditating on? Because as a man thinks in his heart, so is he! (Proverbs 23:7)

I want to give you three excellent biblical principles in Christ that will help you live an excellent life! They are:

1. We must live by the Word of God (Matthew 4:4)
2. We must live by the power of the Holy Spirit. (Gal 5:25)
3. We live by faith. (Rom 1:17)

Now understand that living an excellent life in Christ does not mean you will not go through tests, trials, tribulations, troubles and temptations! But as an excellent saint, you have the mind of Christ to get the victory, and to overcome by the blood of the lamb!

Remember that what you have on the inside of you came from God! Listen to the Apostle Paul:

2 Cor 4:7 says, "But we have this treasure in earthen vessels, that the excellency of the power may be of God, and not of us."

What treasure is Paul talking about? I believe he was referring to who we are in Christ, endowed with the power of the Holy Spirit who dwells in us!

So, **number 1.** To live an excellent life, you must live by the Word of God.

Jesus said in John 6:63, "It is the Spirit who gives life; the flesh profits nothing. The words that I speak to you are spirit, and they are life."

If Jesus is the living Word, and his words are spirit and life, and you get more of the Word in you, then you are getting more of Christ in you!

The majority of Christians don't realize the power they have in Christ. As a matter of fact, many people don't confess what the Bible says they are, who they are, and what the Bible says they have.

A wrong confession is a confession of defeat. A right confession is a confession of God's Word which gives us the victory.

If you study the scriptures, you will see that Jesus always confessed who he was, what he came to do, and what his mission and ministry was.

As a matter of fact, Jesus proclaimed 7 times who he was in scripture.
1. I am the bread of life. John 6: 35
2. I am the light of the World. John 8: 12

3. I am the gate. John 10: 7,9
4. I am the good shepherd. John 10: 11,14
5. I am the resurrection and the life. John 11: 25
6. I am the way, the truth and the life. John 14: 6
7. I am the true vine. John 15: 1. 5

Now, I ask you the question: Who are you and what are you confessing? Are you living by the Word or how you feel? Are you living by the Word of the Lord or the word of the world. Are you living by the Word of the Lord or by what you see?

God's word is powerful, and when we apply it to everything that pertains to life and godliness, it will help us to live a victorious and excellent life!

Number 2. To live an excellent life, you must live by the Holy Spirit.

In order to live by the Holy Spirit, you must allow the Holy Spirit to live in you and guide your thoughts and actions.

"But you shall receive power, after that the Holy Spirit is come upon you: and you shall be witnesses unto me both in Jerusalem, and in all Judaea, and in Samaria, and unto the uttermost part of the earth." (Acts 1:8)

The word power in the Greek text is "Dunamis" which means specifically miraculous power, ability,

abundance, might, a worker of miracles, strength, violence, might or a wonderful work.
Strong's Talking Greek & Hebrew Dictionary.

So, if you have the power of the Holy Spirit in you, then there is something significant on the inside of you! This is why we must allow the Holy Spirit to live in us and guide our thoughts and actions. Listen to what the Apostle Paul said about living by the spirit and living by the flesh.

Rom 8:5 For those who live according to the flesh set their minds on the things of the flesh, but those who live according to the Spirit, the things of the Spirit. Rom 8:6 For to be carnally minded is death, but to be spiritually minded is life and peace.

The book of Galatians confirms it as well.

Gal 5:24 And those who are Christ's have crucified the flesh with its passions and desires.
Gal 5:25 If we live in the Spirit, let us also walk in the Spirit.

So why do we need to live by the Holy Spirit? Well, the Bible tells us why!

The Holy Spirit reveals things to us - 1 Cor 2:9-10
The Holy Spirit speaks to us - Rev 2:7
The Holy Spirit cries out for the believer - Gal 4:6
The Holy Spirit prays for us -Rom 8:26

The Holy Spirit testifies about Jesus Christ - John 15: 26
The Holy Spirit is a teacher - John 14:26, John 16: 12-14
The Holy Spirit instructs us - Neh 9:20
The Holy Spirit leads and guides us. - John 16:13, Rom 8:14

Number 3. To live an excellent life in Christ we should be living by faith!

Roman 10:17 says, "Faith comes by hearing, hearing by the word of God." So, if faith comes from hearing the word of God, we should have a confession of faith that builds us up.

Did you know that the Bible mentions living by faith at least five times?

Behold, his soul which is lifted up is not upright in him: but the just shall live by his faith.
(Habakkuk 2:4)

For therein is the righteousness of God revealed from faith to faith: as it is written, the just shall live by faith.
(Romans 1:17)

But that no man is justified by the law in the sight of God, it is evident for the just shall live by faith.
(Galatians 3:11)

I am crucified with Christ: nevertheless I live; yet not I, but Christ lives in me: and the life which I now live in the flesh I live by the faith of the Son of God, who loved me, and gave himself for me.
(Galatians 2:20)

Now the just shall live by faith: but if any man draw back, my soul shall have no pleasure in him.
(Hebrews 10:38)

Faith is a very important doctrine in the Bible. It is also a very important virtue in the life of the believer. The book of Hebrews shows us the excellency of faith and how those who walked by faith pleased God. Let's read!

Heb 11:1 Now faith is the substance of things hoped for, the evidence of things not seen.
Heb 11:2 For by it the elders obtained a good report.
Heb 11:3 Through faith we understand that the worlds were framed by the word of God, so that things which are seen were not made of things which do appear.
Heb 11:4 By faith Abel offered unto God a more excellent sacrifice than Cain, by which he obtained witness that he was righteous, God testifying of his gifts: and by it he being dead yet speaketh.
Heb 11:5 By faith Enoch was translated that he should not see death; and was not found, because God had translated him: for before his translation he had this testimony, that he pleased God.

Heb 11:6 But without faith it is impossible to please him: for he that cometh to God must believe that he is, and that he is a rewarder of them that diligently seek him.

Heb 11:7 By faith Noah, being warned of God of things not seen as yet, moved with fear, prepared an ark to the saving of his house; by the which he condemned the world, and became heir of the righteousness which is by faith.

These are only a few examples, but as we see, living and walking by faith is so important, and living an excellent life is not a skill, it is an attitude for life.

Vince Lombardi that great hall of fame coach said, "Perfection may not be attainable, but if chase perfection, we can catch excellence!

Living an excellent life in Christ will change your life. It will change the way you think, the way you serve, and even the way you work on your job!

Someone once said that the will to win, the desire to succeed, the urge to reach your full potential, these are the keys that will unlock the door to personal excellence!

As we can see, doing all things in a spirit of excellence unto the LORD is very important. Paul in Philippians chapter 1, wrote to a church and shared a few things with them about being excellent in Philippians chapter 1. Let's read it.

Phi 1:8 For God is my witness, how greatly I long for you all with the affection of Jesus Christ.
Phi 1:9 And this I pray, that your love may abound still more and more in knowledge and all discernment,
Phi 1:10 that you may approve the things that are excellent, that you may be sincere and without offense till the day of Christ,
Phi 1:11 being filled with the fruits of righteousness which are by Jesus Christ, to the glory and praise of God.

The Apostle Paul understood that excellence was important and shared it with one of the churches he established!

When Moses was given the commandment to build the tabernacle, which was a dwelling place for God among his people. The LORD told him, "Make sure you build it according to the pattern or standard I showed you on the mountain."

Exo 25:8 And let them make Me a sanctuary, that I may dwell among them.
Exo 25:9 According to all that I show you, that is, the pattern of the tabernacle and the pattern of all its furnishings, just so you shall make it.

The writer of the book of Hebrews confirms it.
Heb 8:5, "Who serve unto the example and shadow of heavenly things, as Moses was admonished of God when he was about to make the tabernacle: for he

said, see that you make all things according to the pattern showed to you in the mount."

What God was saying is Moses, "I am giving you a heavenly, exceptional, excellent and extraordinary pattern that is in my mind, don't take shortcuts or mess it up!"

As we see, doing all things in excellence unto the LORD is important. God deserves the best in all that we do, and our goal should always be excellence, because he deserves excellence!

When we sin, we miss the mark because we have not met the righteous standards of God, or lived according to that standard.

Now understand that all have sinned and fallen short of the glory of God, but we have been made righteous through the sacrifice and blood of Jesus Christ.

To conclude, let us remember that we serve an excellent God, and it should be our hearts desire to represent him in all of our ways!

Always remember that living a life of excellence not only blesses your life, but it allows us to let our light shine for the LORD, that others may see our good works and glorify God in heaven!

About the Author

Pastor Jamal E. Quinn is the Senior Pastor of Firm Foundation Christian Fellowship in Riverview, FL. He is a native of Louisville, Kentucky and a decorated U.S. Navy veteran of 21 years.

He accepted the call into the ministry and was licensed as a Minister of the Gospel of Jesus Christ in 1999. After retiring from the military in Sep 2005, he returned home to Riverview, a community of Tampa, FL., where the Lord led him to start a community Bible study by faith, preaching, teaching and sharing the Gospel in his neighborhood to family, friends and anyone that had an ear to hear.

In Oct 2007, after faithfully serving in ministry for many years and conducting a Bible study group in his home, the LORD called Pastor Jamal and Prophetess Sheryl Quinn to plant Firm Foundation Christian Fellowship of Jesus Christ in the community of Riverview, Florida with a few faithful Bible study members.

Pastor Quinn is a shepherd, visionary, mentor, and watchman who preaches the Word of God with zeal, passion, power and truth. Pastor Quinn's passion is teaching, exhorting and encouraging men, women and youth to fulfill their God ordained destiny, and to live their lives as examples in Jesus Christ.

Pastor Quinn also worked in the commercial sector for nine years in Information Technology before being called to ministry. He is the author of many other self-published books entitled:

-*"Seven Hindrances to the Blessings of God: Identifying and Removing Hindrances to Spiritual Growth and God's Blessings."*
-*"How Good and How Pleasant it is: The Importance and Power of Unity."*
-*"Speaking the Word of God by Faith."*
-*"The Power of Prayer, Prophecy and Praise."*
-*"R" Daily Devotional: 40 Days of Restoration."*
-*"God's Divine Purpose System: How God manifests divine purpose in your life."*
- *"Closer than a Brother: A scriptural look at friends and friendship."*
-*"Firm Foundation Men's Devotional: 30 Days of Encouragement and Inspiration."*

For additional information on these books, visit the website at https://jamalquinn.com/

He received his Associate of Science Degree in Liberal Arts at Excelsior College, Albany, New York, and his Bachelor of Arts in Pastoral Ministry from South Florida Bible College and Theological Seminary, Deerfield Beach, FL. Pastor Quinn is married to Co-Pastor and 1st Lady Sheryl Quinn. For additional information on Pastor Quinn or Firm Foundation Christian Fellowship, visit https://www.firmfoundationcf.org